W9-CDD-827

Disney and PIXAR Present

SONGBOOK

CONTENTS

SONGS

What fun is in store for you today! This RECORDER FUN™ SONGBOOK
will have you playing the recorder quickly and easily while you learn to play
your favorite songs from Disney's *Toy Story* and *Toy Story 2*.

ISBN 0-634-01650-4

ALSO LOOK FOR *TOY STORY* AND *TOY STORY 2* SOUNDTRACKS
AVAILABLE WHEREVER MUSIC IS SOLD, OR ORDER DIRECT
AT 1-888-WDR-SING, FROM WALT DISNEY RECORDS.

Walt Disney Music Company

DISTRIBUTED BY

7777 W. BLUEMOUND RD. P.O. BOX 13819 MILWAUKEE, WI 53213

Visit Hal Leonard Online at
www.halleonard.com

GETTING STARTED

HOLDING THE RECORDER

Here is how to hold the recorder. The mouthpiece rests on your lower lip, just like a drinking straw, with only a little it actually going inside your mouth. Be sure that all of the finger holes line up on the front of the recorder as shown the picture.

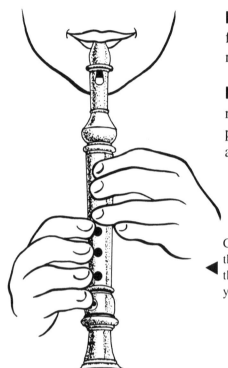

LEFT HAND — The first three fingers of your left hand (the litt finger is not used) play the *top* three holes on the front of th recorder. The thumb of your left hand plays the hole on the back.

RIGHT HAND — The *bottom* four holes are played by yo right-hand fingers. There is no hole for your right-hand thumb play so it can help hold the recorder steady while the other finge are busy playing.

Cover the top three holes with your left-hand fingers and the bottom four holes with your right-hand fingers. The thumb of your left hand covers the hole in the back of your recorder.

MAKING A SOUND

To make a sound on the recorder blow gently into the small opening at the top of the mouthpiece. You can change th sound by covering different holes with your thumb and fingers. For example, when you cover all of the thumb an finger holes you will get a low, quiet sound. When only one or two holes are covered the sound will be higher an much louder.

Here are some tips for getting the best possible sound out of your recorder:

Always blow gently into the mouthpiece — Breathe in and then gently blow into the mouthpiece as if you were sighing or using a straw to blow out a candle. Remember, always blow gently.

Leaks cause squeaks — Play the holes using the pads of your fingers and thumb (not the tips). Press against each hole firmly so that it is completely covered and no air can sneak out. Even a tiny leak of air will change a beautiful tone into a sudden squeak!

Use your tongue to start each tone — Place your tongue against the roof of your mouth just behind your front teeth and start each tone that you play by tonguing the syllable "du" or "too" as you blow gently into the recorder.

PLAYING A TONE

Musical sounds are called *tones*. Every tone has a letter name. *Finger charts* are used to show you exactly which holes should be covered in order to play a particular tone. Each circle on these charts represents one of the holes on your recorder. The thumb hole is represented by the circle to the left of the recorder in the chart.

●   means that you should cover that hole.

○   means that that hole should not be covered but left open.

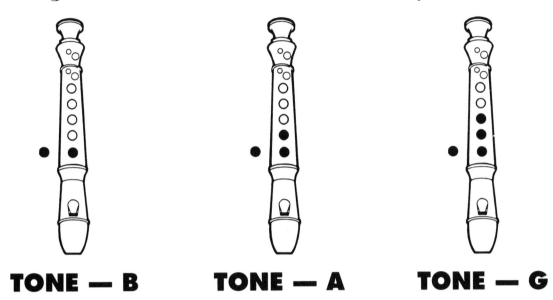

Use these three tones to play "Mary Had A Little Lamb:"

MARY HAD A LITTLE LAMB

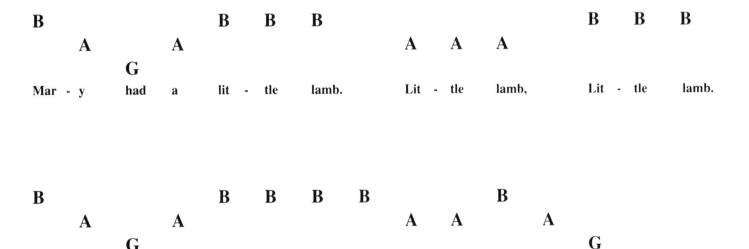

READING MUSIC

Musical notes are an easy way to see everything that you need to know in order to play a song on your recorder

How high or low — Notes are written on five lines that are called a *staff*. The higher a note is written on the staff the higher it will sound.

How long or short — The color of a note (black or white) tells you if it should be played short or long. The black notes in "Mary Had A Little Lamb" are all one beat long (*quarter notes*). The first three white notes in this song are two beats long (*half notes*) and the last note is four beats long (*whole note*).

How the beats are grouped — The two numbers at the beginning of the song (4/4) are called a *time signature*. This time signature tells you that the *beats* in this song are grouped in fours: **1** 2 3 4 **1** 2 3 4 etc. To help you see this grouping, *bar lines* are drawn across the staff to mark each *measure* of four beats. A *double bar* is used to mark the end of the song.

Now here is how "Mary Had A Little Lamb" looks when it is written in musical notes:

MARY HAD A LITTLE LAMB

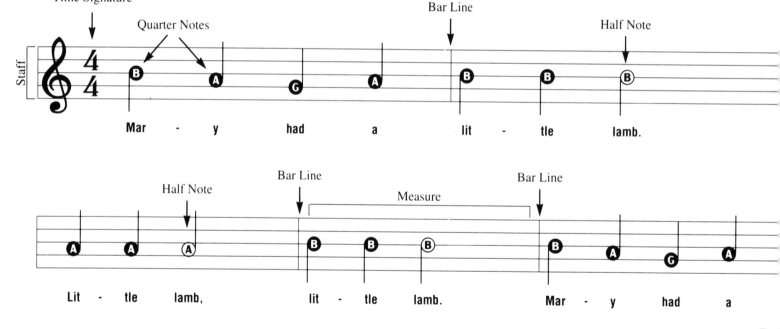

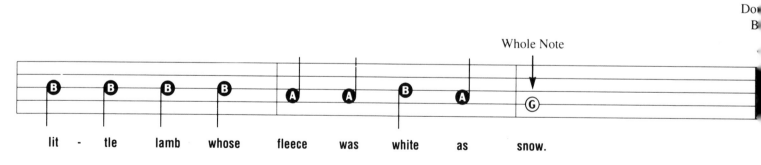

TWO NEW TONES

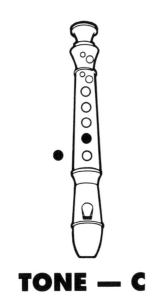

TONE — C

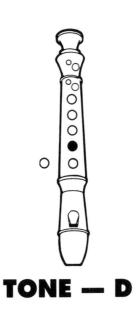

TONE — D

AURA LEE

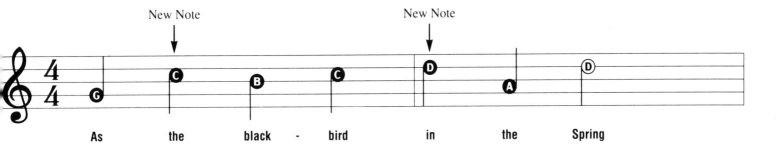

New Note   New Note

G   C   B   C   D   A   D

As   the   black - bird   in   the   Spring

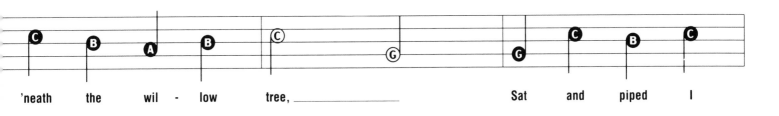

C   B   A   B   C   G   G   C   B   C

'neath   the   wil - low   tree, _____   Sat   and   piped   I

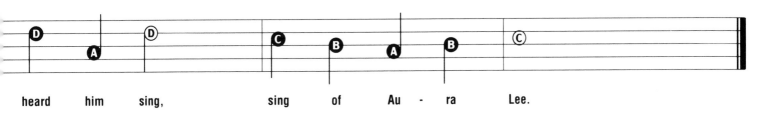

D   A   D   C   B   A   B   C

heard   him   sing,   sing   of   Au - ra   Lee.

USING YOUR RIGHT HAND

"Twinkle, Twinkle Little Star" uses the tone E. As you can see from the fingering chart, you will use three fingers of your left hand and two fingers of your right to play this tone. The thumb hole is only half filled in (◑). This means that you should "pinch" the hole with your thumb so that only a small part of the hole is left open. Pinching is done by bending your thumb so that the thumbnail points directly into the recorder leaving the top of the thumb hole open.

TONE — E

TWINKLE, TWINKLE LITTLE STAR

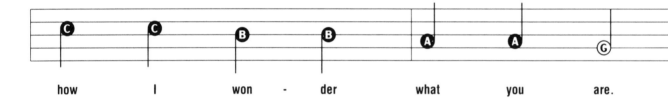

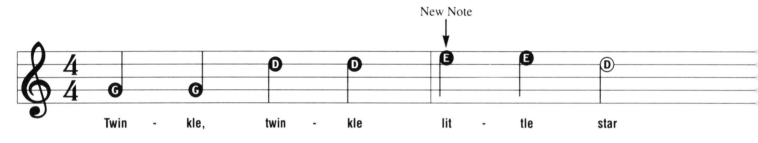

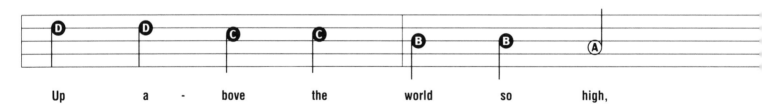

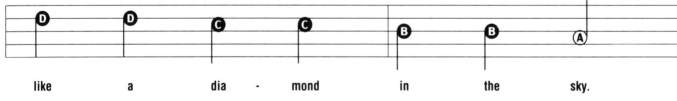

NOTES AND RESTS

In addition to notes that are one, two or four beats long, other values are possible. Also, *rests* are used to indicate when you should *not* play a tone but be silent. The chart on page 7 will help you identify the different notes and rests that are used in this book.

COUNT:

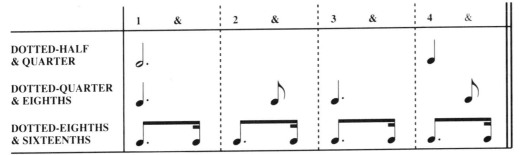

	1 &	2 &	3 &	4 &	NUMBER OF BEATS	REST
WHOLE NOTES					4	
HALF NOTES					2	
QUARTER NOTES					1	
EIGHTH NOTES	(or)				1/2	
& SIXTEENTHS	(or)				1/4	

DOTTED NOTES ARE 1 1/2 TIMES THE NORMAL LENGTH:

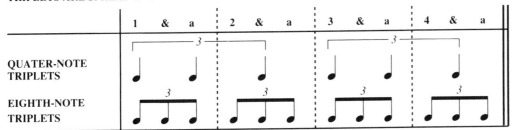

	1 &	2 &	3 &	4 &
DOTTED-HALF & QUARTER				
DOTTED-QUARTER & EIGHTHS				
DOTTED-EIGHTHS & SIXTEENTHS				

TRIPLETS ARE SPREAD EVENLY ACROSS THE BEATS:

	1 & a	2 & a	3 & a	4 & a
QUATER-NOTE TRIPLETS				
EIGHTH-NOTE TRIPLETS				

THIS OLD MAN

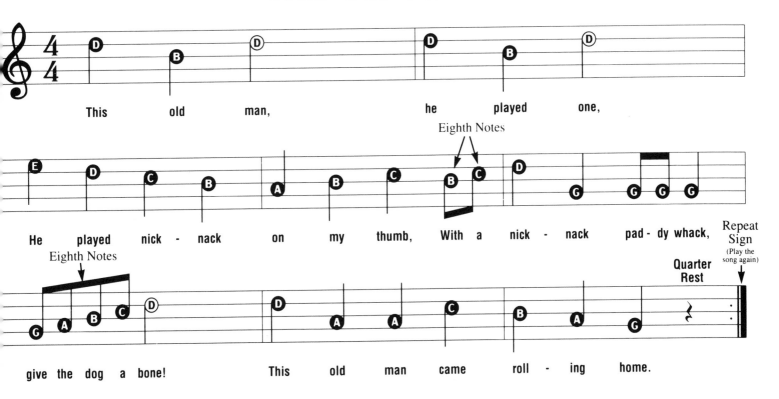

This old man, he played one,

Eighth Notes

He played nick - nack on my thumb, With a nick - nack pad - dy whack,

Eighth Notes

Repeat Sign
(Play the song again)

Quarter Rest

give the dog a bone! This old man came roll - ing home.

FINGERING CHART

Some tones have two names (C♯/D♭, D♯/E♭). These are called enharmonics. Even though enharmonic notes look different, they will sound the same.

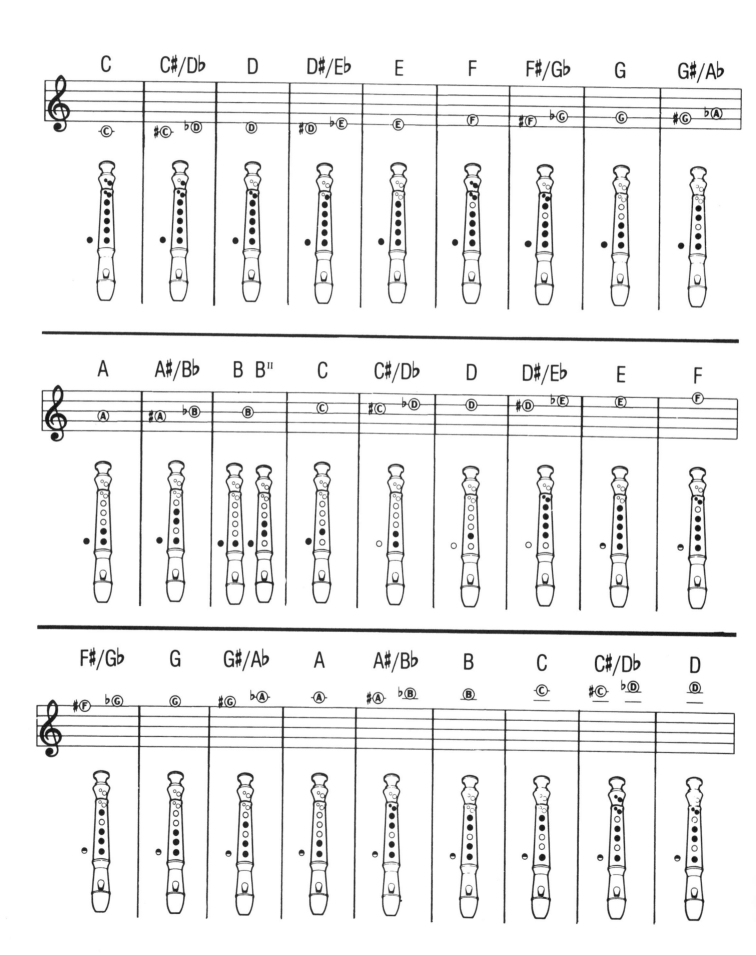

I Will Go Sailing No More

from Walt Disney's TOY STORY

Music and Lyrics by
Randy Newman

Strange Things
from Walt Disney's TOY STORY

Music and Lyrics by
Randy Newman

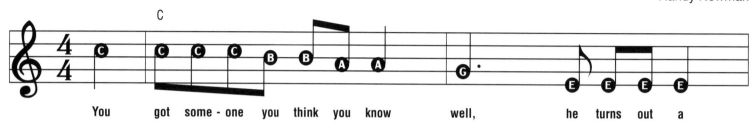

You got some-one you think you know well, he turns out a

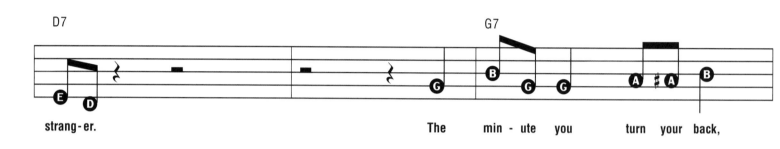

strang-er. The min-ute you turn your back,

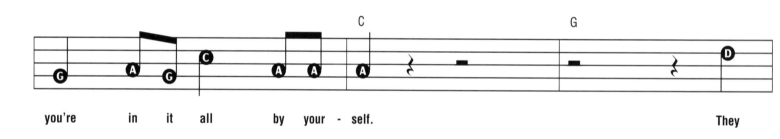

you're in it all by your-self. They

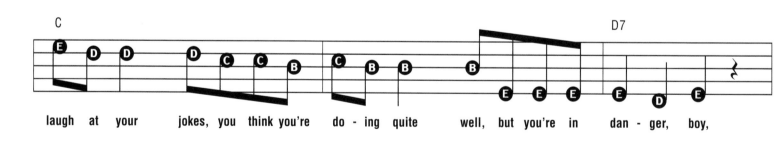

laugh at your jokes, you think you're do-ing quite well, but you're in dan-ger, boy,

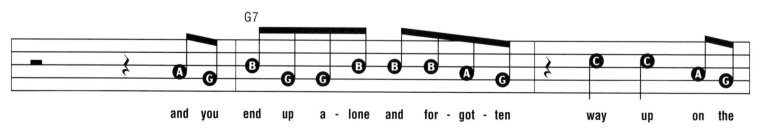

and you end up a-lone and for-got-ten way up on the

When She Loved Me
from Walt Disney Pictures' TOY STORY 2 – A Pixar Film

Music and Lyrics by
Randy Newman

Woody's Roundup
from Walt Disney Picture's TOY STORY 2 – A Pixar Film

Music and Lyrics by
Randy Newman

You've Got a Friend in Me

from Walt Disney's TOY STORY
from Walt Disney Pictures' TOY STORY 2 – A Pixar Film

Music and Lyrics by
Randy Newman

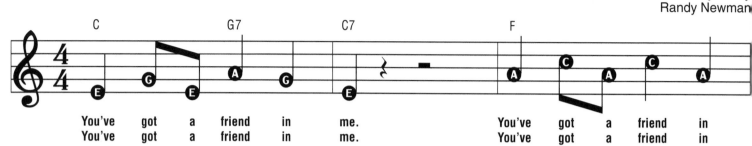

You've got a friend in me. You've got a friend in
You've got a friend in me. You've got a friend in

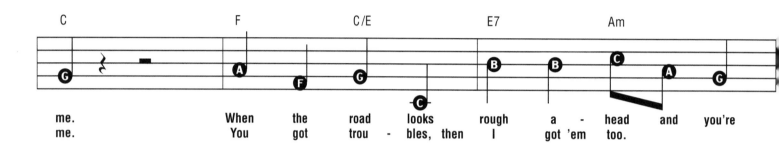

me. When the road looks rough a - head and you're
me. You got trou - bles, then I got 'em too.

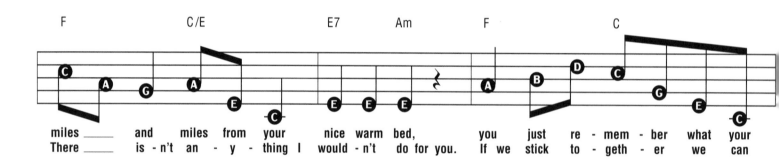

miles ____ and miles from your nice warm bed, you just re - mem - ber what your
There ____ is - n't an - y - thing I would - n't do for you. If we stick to - geth - er we can

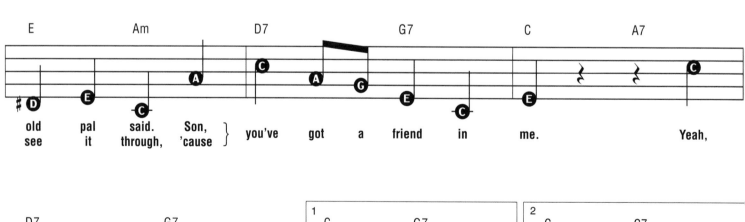

old pal said. Son, you've got a friend in me. Yeah,
see it through, 'cause you've got a friend in me.

you've got a friend in me.

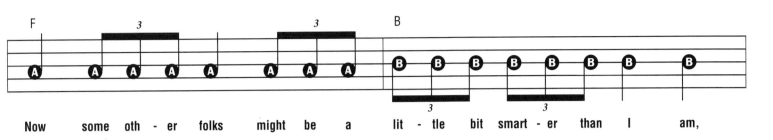

Now some oth - er folks might be a lit - tle bit smart - er than I am,

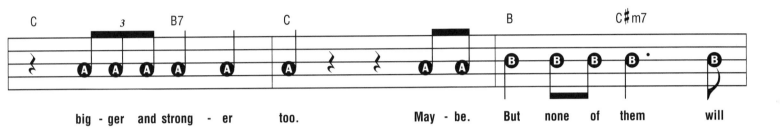

big - ger and strong - er too. May - be. But none of them will

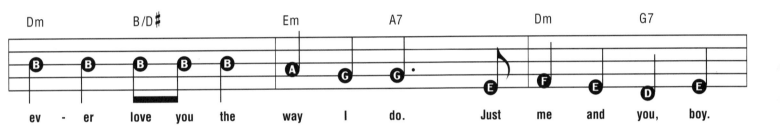

ev - er love you the way I do. Just me and you, boy.

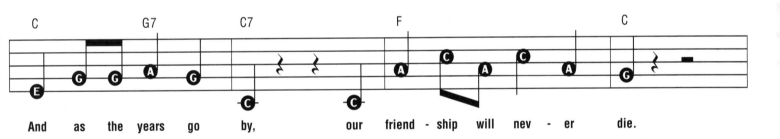

And as the years go by, our friend - ship will nev - er die.

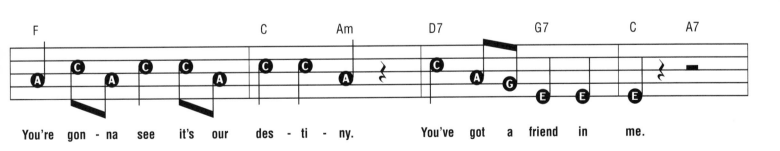

You're gon - na see it's our des - ti - ny. You've got a friend in me.

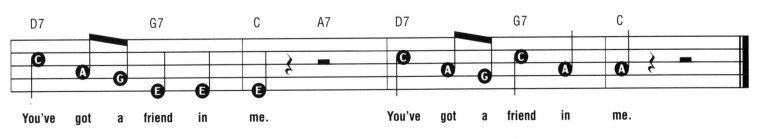

You've got a friend in me. You've got a friend in me.

RECORDER FUN!™

The recorder is a terrific instrument for children to use to learn music. It's lightweight, portable, sounds great, and can be learned quickly and easily. This fun-filled pack features not only a high-quality, long-lasting recorder, but also a songbook that includes simple and easy-to-follow instructions for a young child or beginner plus great coloring pages! Once kids master the basics, they can begin playing their favorite songs from television, films, or characters that they know and love. In no time at all, they'll have learned music basics while having lots of fun!

Recorder Fun! Featuring:

Disney's Aladdin
Pack #00710370

Disney's Beauty and the Beast
Pack #00710359

The Cartoon Songbook
Pack #00824142

The Charlie Brown™ Songbook
Pack #00710039

Christmas Favorites
Pack #00710041

Christmas Songs
Pack #00710372

The Disney Collection
Pack #00710016

Disney 3-Book Collection
(Disney Collection, Disney Favorites,
Princess Collection)
Pack #00710043

Disney Favorites
Pack #00710398
Songbook Only #00710399

Disney Heroes 3-Book Collection
(The Lion King, Toy Story, Disney Collection)
Pack #00710046

Hannah Montana
Pack #00710050

Hide 'Em in Your Heart
Pack #00710036

High School Musical
Pack #00710049

Jonah: A Veggietales® Movie
Pack #00710033

Disney's The Jungle Book
Pack #00710389

Kids' 3-Book Collection
(Recorder Fun, Songs for Kids,
Cartoon Songbook)
Pack #00710044

Disney's Lady and the Tramp
Pack #00710019

Disney's The Lion King
Pack #00710408

Disney's The Little Mermaid
Pack #00710387

My First Hymnal
Pack #00710040

Patriotic Favorites
Pack #00710031

Disney's Pinocchio
Pack #00710363

Disney's Pocahontas
Pack #00710002

Pokémon – 2.B.A. Master
Pack #02500208

Disney's Princess Collection
Pack #00710032

Disney Princess 3-Book Pack
(Beauty and the Beast, Little Mermaid,
Disney's Princess Collection)
Pack #00710045

Disney's Snow White
and the Seven Dwarfs
Pack #00710358

Songs for Kids
Pack #00710393

The Sound of Music®
Pack #00710355

Disney's The Tigger Movie
Pack #00710027

The Toy Story Collection
Pack #00710028

Big Idea's VeggieTales®
Pack #00710030

Disney's Winnie the Pooh
Pack #00710017

Worship Songs for Kids
Pack #00710048

HAL•LEONARD® CORPORATION
7777 W. BLUEMOUND RD. P.O. BOX 13819 MILWAUKEE, WI 53213

Visit Hal Leonard Online at **www.halleonard.com**

Availability and content subject to change without notice.
Not all titles available for export.

Disney characters and artwork © Disney Enterprises, Inc.

0308

The Disney HEROES COLLECTION

Easy arrangements of 14 Disney songs, including:

Beauty and the Beast

Circle of Life

Hakuna Matata

A Whole New World

Woody's Roundup

You've Got a Friend in Me

This Bonus Recorder Fun!™ Pac includes everything you need to teach yourself recorder. In no tim at all, you'll be playing your favorite Disney songs.

THIS PACK INCLUDE

- **RECORDER**
  High quality beginner's recorder with the feel and tuning of a pro model.

- **THREE SONGBOOKS WITH INSTRUCTIONS**
  Easy versions of everyone's favorite Disney songs, plus complete instructions and fingering chart. All in E-Z Play® notation!

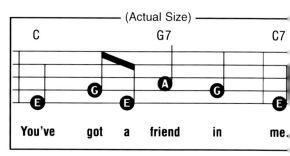

IT'S EASY!
EVEN IF YOU'VE NEVER PLAYED BEFORE!

RECORDER FUN! is a trademark of Hal Leonard Corporation

Disney characters and artwork © Disney Enterprises, Inc.

Printed in USA

ISBN-13: 978-1-4234-184
ISBN-10: 1-4234-1845-X

For Product Information and Comments, Contact:

HAL•LEONARD® CORPORATION
7777 W. BLUEMOUND RD. P.O. BOX 13819 MILWAUKEE, WI 53213

HL00710046